Penguins
On
Leadership

Written and Illustrated

By Lee Sampson

This book is dedicated to everyone I have worked with, laughed with, LinkedIn with and learned from.

To my wife Michelle, children, Arabella, Miles, Cooper and my Mum. I couldn't have done this without you.

Welcome

This is a hand-picked selection of 101 penguin illustrations from my 2022 LinkedIn posts. It follows my first book, Penguins Illustrate Leadership, a little older, wiser, better dressed and sleeker.

The illustrations are unlabelled, grouped into themes in no particular order, inviting you to randomly start at any point and to work forwards or backwards.

The intent is to create a moment with leadership. To relate and offer a fun and thoughtful perspective, leaving you with a smile and something to reflect upon.

Thank you for spending time with the penguins, and I hope you enjoy their company and that they inspire you to make a positive difference today.

I noticed what a good job you
are doing, thank you.
I want you to know it makes a
difference, and we appreciate
you.

It costs nothing but means a lot.

"Yesterday I was clever,
so I wanted to change the world.
Today I am wise, so I am changing myself." -Rumi

A meaningful connection is making the time to care and ask about what is important to others and sharing what is important to you

byLeeSampson

Empathy is critical because it helps strengthen connections which will help keep a team together during challenging times.

byLeeSampson

Developing your empathy as a leader helps
you get better at reading the signs.

byLeeSampson

Setting goals that reward working together
encourages the behaviour of working cohesively,
in unison in the same direction.

byLeeSampson

When work and purpose align, you find the heart.

byLeeSampson

In leadership, bringing out the best of people
starts with seeing them as a person first.

byLeeSampson

The temperature of your leadership defines the
user experience.

byLeeSampson

Leadership is appreciating how people experience
their time at work has a wider impact.

Everyone has a unique story. If you want to get to know someone as a person first, you need to make time to hear and learn their story.

The best leadership is inclusive, creating a safe
space for everyone.

"It's better to change an opinion than to persist with the wrong one" - Socrates

byLeeSampson

byLeeSampson

Be the change...

Work besties, making morning's bearable since
forever.

There is an easy way and a hard way to find
out about mistakes.

byLeeSampson

Words without actions are like planting
flowers and not watering them.

byLeeSampson

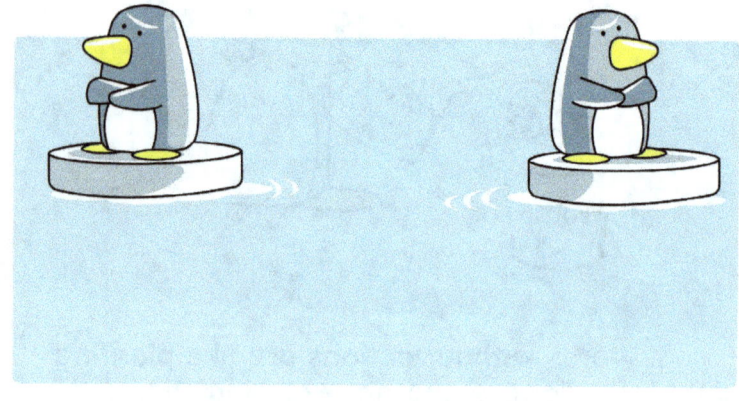

Waiting for the other person to agree you are right.

How you speak to the team is how the Team
will speak to the customers.

Beware of building a team of mirrors. It may
look nice to you, but it's not as strong.

People don't follow a job title.

They follow your actions.

Insisting others be like you is not developing
their potential.

How not to deliver bad news.

"That which is not good for the beehive
cannot be good for the bees".
-Marcus Aurelius

byLeeSampson

Overcome people's natural fear of public humiliation by checking in with people individually.

byLeeSampson

There are few better presents to receive
than a smile you get in return
for giving a genuine, heartfelt compliment.

Are people's reactions towards you a reflection
of your reactions towards them?

byLeeSampson

It's often worth the effort.

Complimenting an introvert in public.

byLeeSampson

Few algorithms can calculate faster than an
Introvert's ability to scan for a safe place to sit
at an event requiring participation.

byLeeSampson

Our Heroes?

I'm listening

Being present and listening is one of the best gifts you can provide.

"If one desires to receive, one must first give.
This is called profound understanding." -Laozi

Being a better communicator is not always
about being better at talking.

It is also about getting better at considering
the impact of your words.

Even if the intent is the same,
the words we use leave a lasting impact.

byLeeSampson

Sometimes, to be heard, you need to address the elephant in the room first.

byLeeSampson

The winning idea is here.

As a Leader, how do you ensure it gets heard?

What remains unsaid under the surface can cause the most damage.

Talking louder doesn't make you more right.

Labelling the behaviour, not the person, allows
space for development.

byLeeSampson

"Educating the mind without educating the heart is no education at all." - Aristotle

It makes more sense and is more beautiful
when all the pieces aren't the same colour.

Leadership presence is like sunscreen:
None or not enough can cause real harm.
With too much, it becomes a slippery mess, gets
in your eyes, and it becomes difficult to get a
proper grip on anything.

byLeeSampson

Adding "fun" as part of your framework will alleviate stress, strengthen team bonds, increase engagement and build fond memories.

byLeeSampson

A culture without diversity (including thoughts)
is limited in what it can create, like a guitar
with only one string.

Leadership should strive to bring people
together.

byLeeSampson

It should not feel like a race to answer questions quickly.

byLeeSampson

Culture helps keep us together.

byLeeSampson.

Setting an expectation to always wear a smile at work masks opportunities to have a genuinely supportive culture.

byLeeSampson

Resentment will demolish any team culture,
no matter who or what the target is.

Culture can be saved or given life by the leader
living and role modelling the values.

byLeeSampson

A workplace that invites people's hopes, dreams and passions in with them helps people bring their hearts to work.

byLeeSampson

There is a gap between
where we are and where we
want to be.

byLeeSampson

Does your process fit people, or do people have
to fit your process?

byLeeSampson

byLeeSampson

This is not
personal,
it's business.

That's not how we
are about to
experience it.

"If you do not change direction, you may end
up where you are heading".
-Lao Tzu

byLeeSampson

Somedays...

Finding the balance keeps everyone level.

byLeeSampson

Getting what you want is less than half of the
leadership equation.

byLeeSampson

Motivating people with fear switches the focus
to you and away from the customer.

byLeeSampson

It's an oversight to think that everyone's idea of a reward is the same.

byLeeSampson

"Education is an ornament in prosperity and a refuge in adversity."
Aristotle

The power of books.

Purpose beats distraction.

A well-thought-out and balanced calendar that includes breaks can help reduce the feeling of not having enough time in a week to get everything done.

byLeeSampson

Having a visual version of your to-do list helps you free up mental real estate, ensures priorities are completed and provides a feel-good boost when items are checked off.

byLeeSampson

Too many meetings can start to impact their effectiveness.

byLeeSampson

It's much easier to eat spaghetti with the right tools. Are you equipping people with the best tools for the job?

byLeeSampson

ideas

imagination

passion

"Don't you know yet?
It is your light that lights the World." -Rumi

New Idea

Response

A natural response to 'new' and 'perceived threats' can be the same.

byLeeSampson

Acknowledging and connecting with people's differing unconscious biases helps them manage through change.

byLeeSampson

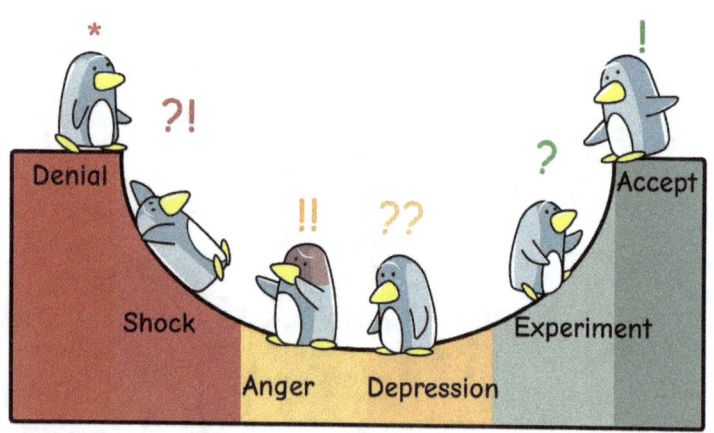

Helping your team understand the change curve and constantly checking in with them is crucial when managing through change.

byLeeSampson

Without perspective, fear can be a very
compelling reason not to move forward.

byLeeSampson

Coaching is both providing the knowledge and
being present to identify the holes.

KNOWLEDGE

EXPERIENCE

"The only source of knowledge is experience".
Albert Einstein

byLeeSampson

It is safer and more productive to learn in a framework that includes support, rather than in an environment of fear and panic.

byLeeSampson

Growth takes time.

It's not about getting stuck. It's who you are
keeping stuck with you that matters.

byLeeSampson

Personal development without support is like teaching someone to drive by only giving them the Car Manual and the Road-Code.

byLeeSampson

It takes more than just dipping your toes in the water to swim with your team.

First Meeting.

byLeeSampson

The difference between feeling like you are in control and how it is received by the team is a matter of perspective.

byLeeSampson

The experience and trust that can be gained
from sharing the skillsets to address challenges
benefit the team, their leader and the customers.

byLeeSampson

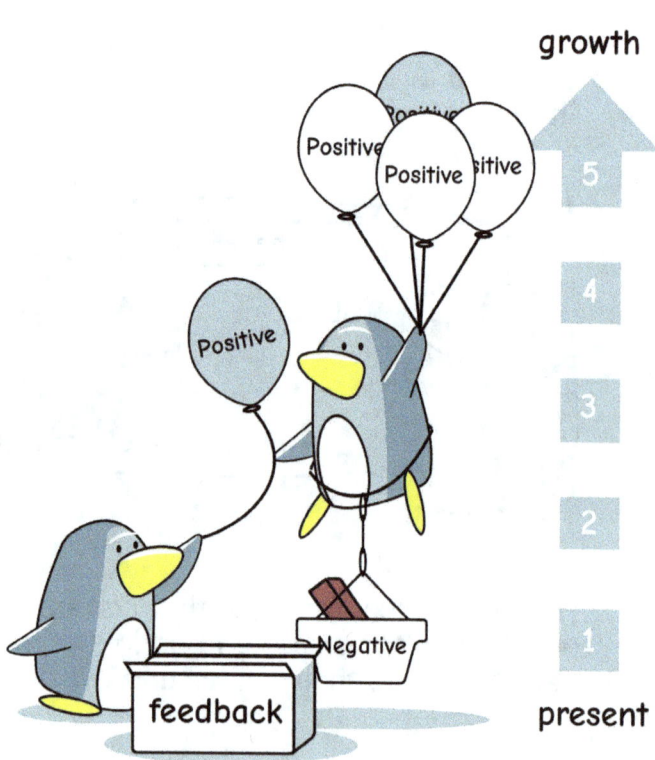

Feedback is like salt and sugar. Putting it in the right place and in the right amounts matters.

byLeeSampson

Feedback allows you to balance the scales of what is being asked of each other to achieve the job.

byLeeSampson

Actions fight fires, not words.

How long you walk with that pebble in
your shoe is up to you.

byLeeSampson

Experience

"It's your road, and yours alone.
Others may walk it with you,
but no one can walk it for you."
-Rumi

We wish you a...

Thank you

Abbie O Adele D Adrian P Al Alexander D Alexander P Althea N Ana W Andrew B Andrew B Anita F Anna K Anna V Anne B Anne J Anne Q Anya F Ariana T Ashley M Baljit K Barney A Bex A Bex P Bhavna P Boopathy S Brendon A Brydee C Byron K Carl F Carl G Carlos M Carmel C Catherine H Chris H Chris K Chris P Chris T Christian S Christy L Christine H Craig P Graig R Colleen T Anne Q Dan B Daniel L Darcella H Darrel T David B David K David P David S Deborah T Deepak S Deshan Dylan B Eddie M Elisabeth D Emily G Emma D Emma N Erena R Eric Erin E Erin W Ernelle O Fiona S Fiona S Frances M Frances T Gagan S Gareth T Garth B Gayle C Gerald N Graham W Greg R Guy S Haakon B Hannah C Harry P Helena S Hrvoje B Ione Jaclyn James L James M James T James W Jamie B Janice K Jay T Jay W Jenny E Jess S Jo C Joanna P John C Jonathan S Joni P Josh D Joshua S Juanita S Jules G Justine S Jyothi S Kalvin G Kano T Karen F Karen O Karl B Karl T Kerryn L Kevin W Kieran M Krissy W Kylie Lauren W Laxmi S Lee M Lenny H Lenny N Lesley M Lincoln N Lisa C Lisa K Lisa M Lison M Liston P Liz G Liz L Lucas A Lwazi T Lynsay G Madeline T Malama M Manaaki B Marcus N Marie B Mark P Mark T Marlene B Matt Matt A Matt S May S Mel C Michael C Michael M Michael S Nadia W Michael W Michela B Michelle C Michelle P Miles W Moana H Monika S Morgan N Nate R Nate T Ned Nicci G Nicholas D Nick B Nick M Nicole E Nigel P Oliver K Oliver M Ollie H Penese P Pera B Petra D Philippa K Pui Y Rachael P Rachel L Raj K Rebecca T Rebekah T Renaye G Rhoda M Ribhu S Richard T Rob C Roma P Ronaldo F Rosannagh G Rose M Rosemary H Ruta J Rux I Sabrina S Saji J Sam I Sam P Sarah D Sean T Shamal C Shanice R Sharon H Sharyn C Shelly G Sherryl P Simon B Sophie C Siobhan G Sky A Solomon B Sophie C Stephanie C Steve S Sue R Sukanya Susan B Tania H Tara D Tarah A Tavian J Tayne F Teagan-Alix B Terrence H Tetaa A Thor B Tim C Tim P Tina B Tina T Todd S Tom M Tracy C Trudy B Tyler K Vaughan W Veronique P Wendy K Wesley H Zac

fin